Original title:
Icicle Veil

Copyright © 2024 Swan Charm
All rights reserved.

Author: Paulina Pähkel
ISBN HARDBACK: 978-9916-79-864-5
ISBN PAPERBACK: 978-9916-79-865-2
ISBN EBOOK: 978-9916-79-866-9

Gaze of the Glaciers

In the still of the frozen night,
Stars twinkle with a silver light.
Mountains loom in silent grace,
Ancient echoes in this place.

Whispers of the icy breeze,
Carry tales of countless freeze.
Crystals glimmer, sharp and clear,
Nature's art, both stark and dear.

Footprints fade on powdered snow,
Wonders hidden, soft and slow.
Snowflakes dance in chilly air,
A world untouched, beyond compare.

Glimmers of a time long past,
Moments caught, forever cast.
In the depths of frozen blue,
Life and death in every hue.

At dawn, the glaciers softly gleam,
A canvas brushed from nature's dream.
Look closely, you may just find,
The stories of a heart entwined.

Delicate Fringes

In twilight's soft embrace we find,
Gentle whispers swirl and wind.
Petals brush against the air,
Fringes dance with beauty rare.

The moonlight spills on silken threads,
Where every dream and hope spreads.
A canvas woven with such grace,
Delicate fringes in a place.

Amidst the sighs of evening's glow,
A melody in breezes flow.
Fragile moments, hearts entwined,
A tapestry of love designed.

As shadows deepen, colors blend,
Where night and day begin to bend.
In silence, secrets softly weave,
The art of life we dare believe.

Each breath a note in nature's song,
In harmony, we all belong.
Delicate fringes mark the way,
Guiding souls till break of day.

Frozen Lace

Winter whispers through the trees,
Crafting lace from frosty breeze.
Crystal patterns on the ground,
In the stillness, beauty found.

Each flake a story, pure and bright,
Sparkling under pale moonlight.
A quilt of white, serene and vast,
Frozen lace, a moment cast.

Branches draped in silver fine,
Nature's art, a grand design.
Every twinkle, every gleam,
Frosted whispers in a dream.

Beneath the weight of icy breath,
Life pauses, dancing with death.
In this hush, we come to see,
Frozen lace, a memory.

As morning breaks, a soft embrace,
Sunrise melts the frosty space.
Yet in our hearts, forever stays,
The beauty of that wintry phase.

Gleaming Cascade

A waterfall of silver light,
Dancing droplets in their flight.
Nature's joy, a wild song,
Gleaming cascade, where dreams belong.

Rushing waters, swift and free,
Carving paths through ancient trees.
Mirrored sun on rippling streams,
Waking us from sleepy dreams.

With every splash, a tale unfolds,
Whispers told in silver folds.
Eager hearts gather 'round to see,
The magic of this symmetry.

In twilight's glow, reflections play,
Chasing shadows far away.
Within the mist, life's essence flows,
Gleaming cascade, where wonder grows.

The night may call, the stars provoke,
But still, the spirits of the brook.
Forever bound, in nature's clasp,
The gleaming cascade, our hearts grasp.

Suspended Beauty

A moment held in time's embrace,
Captured breath and softest grace.
In twilight's hush, the world stands still,
Suspended beauty, hearts fulfill.

The quiet sigh of evening's glow,
Soft shadows dance, a gentle show.
Every heartbeat synchronizes,
In this realm, love recognizes.

Above the fields where silence grows,
Suspended laughter gently flows.
A fleeting glance that lingers long,
Melodies of an unplayed song.

The canvas stretched between two worlds,
Where dreams take flight and fate unfurls.
In fragile glimmers, love defined,
Suspended beauty, hearts enshrined.

With each new dawn, we must let go,
Yet carry remnants in our glow.
The perfect pause in life's ballet,
Suspended beauty lights the way.

Veils of Liquid Diamond

Glistening drops in soft twilight,
Dancing shadows, a pure delight.
Each droplet twirls, a wondrous sight,
Veils of liquid diamond, shining bright.

Waves of shimmer, like whispered dreams,
Reflecting all in silvery beams.
Nature's grace, or so it seems,
In the night, where magic teems.

Beneath the stars, the world feels new,
Cascading light, a gentle hue.
Each moment held, as if in cue,
Connected hearts, forever true.

In stillness found, the air so clear,
Everlasting joy, drawing near.
With every breath, we cast out fear,
Liquid diamonds, oh so dear.

In this realm, time pauses to play,
Moments stretch, in soft ballet.
With gleaming veils, we drift away,
To dream beneath the starry sway.

Twilight's Frozen Kiss

When dusk descends and shadows meet,
A chill sweeps through, a soft retreat.
The world adorned in icy sheet,
Twilight's frozen kiss, bittersweet.

Pale moonlight casts a silver glow,
Whispers of warmth in the crisp below.
Each breath fogs as cold winds blow,
Nature sleeps, quiet as the snow.

Hushed feelings linger, time stands still,
In frosty air, we find the thrill.
Hearts entwined, we climb the hill,
Wrapped in dreams, a winter's will.

Glistening paths, with sparkles laid,
Through frozen woods, our fears just fade.
In this embrace, our hopes cascade,
Into the magic twilight made.

The silent night's sweet lullaby,
Under starlit skies, we'll softly lie.
With frozen dreams, our spirits fly,
In twilight's kiss, we learn to sigh.

Whispering Cold

A shiver dances through the trees,
Gentle whispers on the breeze.
In the hush, the world agrees,
Whispering cold, with quiet ease.

Chill of night wraps us in grace,
A world transformed in this embrace.
Every breath, a frosted trace,
In silence still, we find our place.

Echoes linger, soft and near,
Capturing moments, crystal clear.
In the cold, our hearts draw near,
Whispering secrets, none to fear.

Each frosty sigh, a tale retold,
In wintry realms, where dreams unfold.
Embracing warmth in stories bold,
Through whispering cold, we feel consoled.

With silver stars that softly shine,
In this realm where you are mine.
We'll dance beneath constellations fine,
To the rhythm of the cold divine.

Frosty Reverberation

Echoes of frost in the morning light,
A world adorned in brilliance bright.
Each note strikes a chord, pure and right,
Frosty reverberation takes flight.

Crystal notes linger in the air,
Harmonies float, a sweet affair.
Nature's song, without a care,
Melodies swirling everywhere.

In stillness found, we dance along,
To winter's tune, we both belong.
With every breath, we sing our song,
In frosty air where dreams are strong.

As sunbeams touch the silvered ground,
Beauty unfolds, where love is found.
In this moment, hearts are bound,
With frosty echoes, hope resound.

In every whisper, nature plays,
Creating bliss on winter days.
Frosty reverberation sways,
Entwining souls in soft arrays.

Gentle Crystals of January

The snowflakes fall, so soft and white,
Blanketing the earth, a pure delight.
Each crystal unique, a shimmering show,
Whispers of winter in the gentle glow.

Footsteps crunch on powdery ground,
Echoes of silence, a serene sound.
Frozen branches dance in the breeze,
Nature's artwork, simple to please.

Cold air kisses cheeks with a chill,
Fires crackle softly, hearts to fill.
Hot cocoa warms hands with sweet embrace,
Contentment blooms in this frosty space.

Wrapped in layers, we venture outside,
Chasing the sun, where shadows slide.
With laughter and joy, we embrace the day,
Gentle crystals guide our playful way.

The Dance of Frozen Light

Sunrise breaks with colors bright,
Dancing beams in frozen light.
Icicles cling like crystal spears,
Glistening bright through winter years.

Snowflakes twirl in joyful flight,
Whirling softly, pure delight.
Nature's rhythm, calm and clear,
A symphony that all can hear.

Frosty whispers on the air,
Magic drifts without a care.
Each flurry tells a tale untold,
Of winter's wonders, bright and bold.

Step by step, our shadows merge,
In tranquil paths where dreams converge.
Under the sky, so vast and free,
We dance to winter's melody.

Frosted Secrets

Beneath the snow, a world asleep,
Secrets buried, safe to keep.
Frosted leaves hold whispers tight,
Guarding stories from the night.

Moonlight sparkles on the ground,
In the stillness, peace is found.
Softly breathing, the winter air,
Promises linger everywhere.

Hidden paths in swirling white,
Navigating by soft twilight.
Footprints lead where few have trod,
In frost-kissed realms, we find a nod.

Nature's canvas, blank and bare,
Cradles dreams beyond compare.
Through the frost, we hear the call,
To uncover secrets, one and all.

Iridescent Winter Shadows

In twilight's glow, shadows dance,
Iridescent hues take their chance.
Frosted edges sparkle bright,
A magical touch of winter's light.

The trees stand tall in grand display,
Casting silhouettes at the end of day.
Each branch a story, every line,
A tapestry woven, a design divine.

Whispers of chill caress the night,
As stars emerge, a brilliant sight.
With every glimmer, dreams ignite,
In the heart of winter's light.

Beneath the moon, we find our peace,
In shadows where all worries cease.
Iridescent moments, pure and true,
Winter's wonder welcomes you.

Frosted Whispers

In the still of winter's breath,
Silent voices softly weave,
Tales of snowflakes' gentle kiss,
Nature's secrets we believe.

Frozen echoes drift and sway,
Carried on the frosty air,
Whispers linger, cold and bright,
Frosted dreams beyond compare.

Trees adorned in icy lace,
Stand as sentinels of light,
Glowing under the pale moon,
Hushed beneath the stars so bright.

Chill of night, a tender balm,
Painting worlds in crystal hues,
Memories wrapped in frosted calm,
Nature's art in winter's muse.

Every flake a story spun,
Dancing softly on the breeze,
Frosted whispers, softly sung,
Echo gently through the trees.

Crystal Draperies

Morning wakes with gleaming rays,
Curtains drawn of glimmering frost,
Nature's touch in bright display,
A beauty found, never lost.

Fields of white, a soft embrace,
Crystal draperies, pure and wide,
Cascading down from heaven's grace,
Joyful whispers, winter's pride.

Treetops shimmer, diamonds glow,
Every branch a work of art,
Glistening bright, a world aglow,
Nature's beauty warms the heart.

Footsteps crunch on frosty ground,
Echoes swell in morning's light,
Lost in wonder, peace is found,
In this realm of sheer delight.

With each glance, a spark ignites,
Crystal draperies, draped in gold,
Moments captured, purest sights,
A winter's tale forever told.

Shimmering Chill

A breath of winter in the air,
Softly wraps the world around,
Every moment, crisp and rare,
In the hush, a soothing sound.

Shimmering chill, a dance divine,
Frosted grace upon the land,
Nature's artwork, pure design,
Crafted gently by a hand.

Blankets white on fields of green,
Sparkling under morning's glow,
A landscape ripe, serene, unseen,
Whispers move in silent flow.

Golden rays through branches weave,
Lighting up the snowy scene,
In this magic, we believe,
Moments fleeting, yet they glean.

With a sigh, the day unfolds,
Wrapped in warmth beneath the chill,
Stories of the ice, retold,
In the heart, a quiet thrill.

Glistening Filaments

Threads of light in frosty air,
Glistening filaments of white,
Woven on the canvas fair,
A tapestry of pure delight.

Twinkling in the morning sun,
Nature's jewels, bright and bold,
Each a secret, every one,
Whispers of the winter's cold.

Beneath the branches, shadows play,
Frosted patterns, rich and deep,
In the silence, dreams will sway,
Glistening filaments that keep.

Winding through the icy trees,
Magic lingers in the breeze,
Each step leaves a gentle trace,
Captured moments, time at ease.

As the day begins to fade,
Colors shift in dusky light,
Glistening filaments displayed,
A winter's dream, a pure delight.

Winter's Silken Cloak

Snowflakes dance in the hush of night,
Blanketing earth in purest white.
Silent whispers embrace the trees,
Nature rests, wrapped in a dream's breeze.

Stars twinkle like diamonds up high,
Under the vast, velvet sky.
Footprints trace stories on frosted ground,
In the stillness, serenity is found.

Fires crackle, inviting and warm,
As the world outside transforms its form.
Cups of cocoa, sweetened delight,
Gather us close on this cozy night.

Icicles hang like crystal tears,
Telling tales of winter's years.
With every breath, a cloud of white,
In winter's grasp, we find delight.

Nature's lullaby whispers low,
As time drifts softly like fresh-fallen snow.
In the calm, our hearts take flight,
Wrapped in winter's silken light.

Frozen Elegance

Beneath the moon's soft, silver glow,
Each branch wears frost like jewels in tow.
Glittering fields of ice and snow,
A tranquil beauty in every flow.

The wind's gentle sigh has secrets to share,
Softening whispers float through the air.
Silver crystals adorn the night,
A frozen elegance, pure and bright.

Pine trees stand tall, robed in white,
Guarding the dreams that dance out of sight.
Each breath, a ribbon of shimmering mist,
A winter's magic that can't be missed.

Skaters glide on the glassy lake,
Leaving behind a joyful wake.
With laughter ringing, hearts entwined,
In frozen elegance, warmth we find.

Nightfall brings a stillness so deep,
As the world wraps itself in a gentle sleep.
In the quiet, wonder transcends,
A frozen elegance that never ends.

Ethereal Frost

Morning light kisses the frosted dew,
Painting the landscape in shades anew.
A blanket of white cloaks the field,
Ethereal frost, a beauty concealed.

Each breath turns into a fleeting cloud,
Nature is silent, serene, and proud.
Whispers of winter carry through air,
A dance of sparkling, crystalline flare.

Branches adorned like a bride in white,
Sparkle and glimmer in soft morning light.
A canvas of dreams stretched far and wide,
In this ethereal world, we abide.

Snowflakes swirl like dancers in flight,
Painting the sky with sheer delight.
Winter's embrace, gentle and soft,
Ethereal frost carries our thoughts aloft.

As day gives way to twilight's call,
Stars unfurl and begin to fall.
In the silence, watch beauty unfurl,
Ethereal frost, our enchanting world.

Lattice of Winter

Through branches bare, the moonlight weaves,
A lattice of winter, where magic breathes.
Each glint and shimmer tells a tale,
Of nights so still, where dreams prevail.

Glistening pathways invite the bold,
Stories of wonder waiting to unfold.
Children laugh as they tumble and play,
In the tapestry of winter's sway.

Frozen lakes mirror the starry skies,
A symphony played by night's lullabies.
Nature holds hands with the chill of air,
In a lattice of winter, beyond compare.

Gentle flakes fall as soft as a sigh,
Whirling and twirling as they float by.
In the chilly embrace of the night,
We gather warmth in the fading light.

With every breath, the hush lingers on,
Under the spell of the winter dawn.
In this lattice of dreams, we are free,
Finding solace in winter's decree.

Chilled Reverie

Whispers ride on icy air,
Beneath the silent, pale moon's glare.
Footprints crisp on virgin snow,
Lost in dreams where cold winds blow.

Frosty breath of night unfolds,
Stories wrapped in winter's folds.
Stars like diamonds in the sky,
Glimmer softly, as time slips by.

Trees stand tall, their branches bare,
Laced with crystals, debonair.
Nature's hush, a gentle sigh,
Moments pass as shadows fly.

Candle glows in windows bright,
Warming hearts in frosty night.
Memories dance, like spirits near,
Echoes linger, soft and clear.

Wrapped in blankets, cozy tight,
Chilled reveries take flight.
In this stillness, dreams reside,
Winter's chill, a tender guide.

Silver Threads of Ice

Morning breaks with frosty light,
In a world of gleaming white.
Silver threads of ice entwine,
Nature's jewels, pure and fine.

Glades adorned in crystal lace,
Each branch holds a fragile grace.
Sunrise splashes warmth anew,
Painting gold on every hue.

Silent whispers weave through trees,
Carried soft on winter's breeze.
Cascades of sparkles in the air,
Magic lingers everywhere.

Footsteps crunch on frozen ground,
In this tranquil space, I'm found.
Nature's silence, calm and deep,
Lulls my heart into sweet sleep.

Evening falls, the stars appear,
In the stillness, I feel near.
Underneath the moonlit skies,
Silver threads of ice arise.

Winter's Ethereal Cloak

Softly draped in white's embrace,
Winter whispers, leaves no trace.
Ethereal cloak, serene and bright,
Blankets earth by day and night.

Snowflakes dance on gentle winds,
Each one tells of where it's been.
Patterns woven, art divine,
Nature sketches in pure line.

Frozen lakes, a glassy sheen,
Reflect the calm, the peaceful scene.
Peace descends like evening's mist,
In this beauty, none exist.

Branches bowed with heavy weight,
Nature holds her breath in fate.
Silent shadows softly creep,
As the world begins to sleep.

Stars flicker, a chilling grace,
In this hush, I find my place.
Wrapped in dreams, gentle and slow,
In winter's ethereal cloak I grow.

Subtle Fractals

Fractals bloom in chilly air,
Whirling shapes, so fine and rare.
Nature paints with icy breath,
Artists dance, defying death.

Patterns form on windows clear,
Tales of winter, drawing near.
As the night begins to fall,
Whispers soften, gently call.

Branch and bough, adorned with frost,
Are the memories that I've lost.
Each design a fleeting trace,
In the silence, find my space.

Snowflakes weave a tapestry,
In this world, just you and me.
Underneath the pale moon's glow,
Subtle fractals start to show.

Time stands still, a gentle pause,
Wrapped in winter's pure applause.
Through the stillness, beauty thrives,
In each fractal, life derives.

Cascades of Chill

Whispers of frost fill the air,
Cascades of chill dance through trees.
Silent streams under ice wear,
Nature's breath, a soft tease.

Snowflakes drift, a timeless flight,
Each unique in frozen grace.
Moonlit nights bring soft delight,
Blanketing the world's embrace.

The world pauses, a tranquil sigh,
With every flake, a hush profound.
In silence, the cold winds cry,
As dreams in winter's grip abound.

Icicles hang like crystal spears,
Guardians of the winter's art.
A symphony of chill appears,
Playing softly on the heart.

Fires flicker, warmth inside,
Against the chill, we gather near.
With every laugh, our hearts bide,
In this season, rich and clear.

Frigid Veils

Veils of frost coat every pane,
Whispers soft upon the night.
Winter's breath, a gentle chain,
Binding dreams in silver light.

Trees adorned with icy lace,
Each bough heavy, stoic, bold.
Nature dons a pristine face,
While stories of cold unfold.

Footprints trace a silent path,
In the snow, memories bloom.
Every step feels like a bath,
In the hush of winter's room.

Stars look down with icy glee,
Twinkling through the vast expanse.
Silent tales from far and free,
As through the night we dance.

With each dawn, new scenes arise,
Frigid veils, a shifting scene.
Nature's canvas prompts our eyes,
In this realm of white serene.

Winter's Gossamer Shroud

A shroud of white o'er all is cast,
Cloaked in whispers, soft and low.
Winter's gossamer holds steadfast,
In the quiet, bare and slow.

Branches bow beneath the weight,
Frozen fingers grasp the sky.
Time itself seems to hesitate,
As dreams in frozen beauty lie.

The dance of flakes begins anew,
Waltzing through the crisp, cool air.
Every flake a world to view,
In silence whispers everywhere.

Crisp sunbeams kiss the morning chill,
Transforming fields to shimmering gold.
Yet the air, though bright, is still,
Winter's story still unfolds.

As evening draws its curtain close,
The stars emerge, a dazzling crowd.
Wrapped in night, the world doze,
Beneath winter's gossamer shroud.

Transparent Lattice

In the stillness, frost takes form,
A transparent lattice weaves.
Nature's quilt, both pure and warm,
Underneath, the earth believes.

Frosted patterns grace the ground,
Every inch a tale to tell.
In this magic, peace is found,
Where the cold embraces well.

The lattice glitters in the light,
Each crystal spark, a fleeting dream.
Casting shadows deep of night,
Where memories seem to gleam.

Through the branches, sunbeams break,
Illuminating the chill's embrace.
Nature breathes, and we partake,
In this woven, wintry grace.

Time flows gently, as if in trance,
In the splendor of this frost.
A fleeting moment, a sublime dance,
As we cherish what we've lost.

Frost-Kissed Marvels

Underneath the morning light,
The world shimmers, pure and bright.
Each tree wears a diamond crown,
Nature's art, in silence, found.

Whispers of the winter's song,
Echo soft, where dreams belong.
The ground sparkles, crystal fair,
Frost-kissed wonders linger there.

In the stillness, magic flows,
As the chilly breeze intows.
Every flake, a story spun,
A fleeting gift 'til day is done.

Breath of winter, crisp and clear,
Holds the warmth of those we hold dear.
In every glance, a world anew,
Frost-kissed marvels, pure and true.

Golden rays begin to gleam,
Dissolving ice, a waking dream.
Yet the memory will remain,
Of frost-kissed wonders, sweet refrain.

Veils of the Eternal Frost

Veils of white dance through the pines,
Holding secrets, ancient signs.
Each breath comes with a silver chill,
Whispered tales the night does fill.

Frozen rivers, pathways wide,
In their grasp, the world does hide.
Wrapped in silence, cold and deep,
Guarding treasures, dreams to keep.

Crystal shadows cloak the trees,
Rustling softly in the breeze.
Nature sleeps beneath the snow,
In her slumber, she will grow.

Stars above like diamonds shine,
As the moon begins to climb.
Veils of frost, a soft embrace,
Cradling night in spectral grace.

As dawn breaks, the frost will fade,
Yet in hearts, its touch is laid.
A moment captured, still and bright,
Veils of frost, a pure delight.

Veils of Glimmering Night

In the hush of twilight's cheer,
Veils of night draw ever near.
Stars like gems graced the dark,
Kindling dreams, igniting spark.

Waves of silver, shadows blend,
Secrets whispered without end.
Moonscape dances on the lake,
Each wave mirrors the heart's ache.

Crisp air carries tales untold,
In this realm, the brave and bold.
Night wraps 'round like a soft shroud,
Breath of freedom, soft and loud.

Through the darkness, glimmers shine,
Every heartbeat feels divine.
Wrapped in veils, we find our way,
Guided gently by the sway.

Night's embrace, a tender friend,
Where all longing hearts can mend.
Veils of glimmer, night's delight,
In their arms, we find our light.

Fiery Heart in a Frozen World

In the midst of winter's chill,
A heartbeat echoes, strong and still.
A fiery heart defies the cold,
In passion's warmth, its tale unfolds.

Snowflakes dance, a swirling waltz,
Yet love's flame beneath the vaults.
Every spark ignites the night,
Chasing shadows, sharing light.

Frosty breath, a heated sight,
In this world, we seek our flight.
Through each trial, hand in hand,
Together, we forever stand.

In the frozen, stark terrain,
Love's fierce warmth will still remain.
With every step, the fire grows,
In our hearts, a steady glow.

As seasons change, we'll still endure,
A fiery heart that's bold and pure.
In a frozen world, we'll thrive,
With flames of love, eternally alive.

Nature's Delicate Frosting

Whispers of winter grace the ground,
Sparkling crystals all around.
Each blade of grass in silver dressed,
Nature's beauty, pure and blessed.

Trees adorned in frosty white,
Glistening softly in the light.
Birds take flight, a playful show,
In the chill, they dance and flow.

Footprints left in snow so deep,
Silent secrets, quiet sleep.
Nature weaves her gentle art,
Frosted wonders, pure of heart.

Morning light begins to break,
Crisp and clear, it starts to wake.
Every breath a cloud of mist,
In this beauty, we exist.

Winter's tale, a fleeting dream,
As sunlight's rays begin to gleam.
Nature's frost, a soft embrace,
A moment found in time and space.

Frosted Fantasia

Dancing shadows on the ground,
Frost and icicles abound.
Dreamlike visions, cold and bright,
Wrapped in winter's pure delight.

Silver strands of morning dew,
Every glance, a wondrous view.
Nature plays her icy tune,
Beneath the pale and frosty moon.

Whispers of a world at rest,
Cold enchantments, beauty blessed.
Sparkling under sunlight's glow,
Frosted scenes in hush and flow.

A tapestry of white and blue,
Crafted skies, a stunning hue.
Footsteps echo, silence reigns,
In this wonder, joy remains.

Twilight casts a gentle spell,
In this frozen, magic swell.
Nature's brush, it paints so grand,
A frosted dream across the land.

Crystalized Dreams of Winter

As twilight falls and shadows creep,
Winter's secrets softly leap.
Every flake, a tale to tell,
Crystal dreams where spirits dwell.

Frosted streams with glassy flows,
In the hush, a beauty glows.
Feral whispers, winds that sigh,
In this realm where moments fly.

Beneath the stars, the world asleep,
Where memories and silence seep.
Nature's wonders come alive,
In winter's heart, our dreams survive.

Frozen lakes, a glimmer bright,
Reflecting soft and pale moonlight.
Journeys taken, hearts set free,
In this magic, joy we see.

Each breath a mist, a fleeting view,
In winter's grasp, love feels anew.
Frosted dreams begin to gleam,
Held within a silent dream.

Enigmatic Chill

Beneath the frost, a world so still,
Whispers echo, soft and shrill.
Nature cloaked in mystery,
Wrapped in winter's tapestry.

Veils of white on trees do cling,
Silhouettes where shadows sing.
Frozen breath upon the air,
Every moment, rich and rare.

Chill of night, a ghostly dance,
Under stars, in frozen trance.
Each sigh carried by the breeze,
Nature's secrets tease and please.

Crimson leaves, now dusted white,
In the chill, a strange delight.
Hidden paths of endless snow,
Lead us where the wild winds blow.

As dawn breaks, the chill may fade,
Yet in our hearts, the dreams cascade.
Enigmatic, winter's grace,
A lingering smile on nature's face.

Chills of Canopy

Beneath the boughs where shadows play,
Whispers of winter greet the day.
Silent snowflakes softly fall,
Nature's breath, a gentle call.

The branches wear their frosty lace,
A quiet world, a tranquil space.
Crystals dance in morning's light,
Chills of canopy take flight.

The air is crisp, the silence deep,
A moment paused, a time to keep.
Life in slumber, beneath the freeze,
A sacred peace, the mind's reprieve.

Yet in this cold, a warmth does bloom,
In heart and soul, dispelling gloom.
With every breath, a promise made,
Chills of canopy won't soon fade.

Embrace the still, let worries cease,
In nature's arms, we find our peace.
Where branches arch in gentle grace,
Chills of canopy, a sweet embrace.

Icy Whirl

In twilight's hush, the dance begins,
A swirling storm, where silence spins.
Frosty tendrils claw the ground,
In icy whirl, a song resounds.

Through swirling flurries, shadows glide,
With every spin, there's nowhere to hide.
Whispered secrets in the night,
Icy whirl, a ghostly flight.

The world transformed in shades of white,
Ethereal beauty, pure delight.
Each flake a story, each gust a tale,
In icy whirl, spirits sail.

Beneath the stars, the cold winds wail,
In frozen realms, we set our sail.
Through whirlwinds wild, we find our way,
An icy maze where dreams can stay.

In frosty air, the heart takes wing,
With every breath, winter's offering.
Icy whirl, a dance of fate,
In crystal realms, we celebrate.

Silken Winter

A soft embrace of flakes that fall,
Whispers sweet, a muffled call.
The world adorned in glistening white,
Silken winter, pure delight.

Each branch a canvas, art displayed,
Gentle hues where light is laid.
In quiet corners, beauty wakes,
Silken winter, the heart it takes.

Dreams wrapped in blankets, warm and tight,
As evening falls, we greet the night.
With every breath, the chill sets in,
Silken winter draws us in.

The moon hangs low, a guardian bright,
Illuminating paths of light.
In frosted fields where silence reigns,
Silken winter, a love unchained.

In this embrace, we find our rest,
Within these moments, we are blessed.
For in the cold, hearts begin to stir,
Silken winter, a gentle blur.

Drifting Frost

As dawn awakes with rosy hue,
The world adorned in crystalline view.
Each breath a cloud in morning's chill,
Drifting frost, the heart does fill.

The landscape glimmers, pure and bright,
In soft caress of winter's light.
Whispers of frost on blades of green,
Drifting frost, a silent scene.

With every step, a crunch beneath,
The earth wrapped tight in frosty sheath.
A tapestry, nature's art displayed,
Drifting frost, where dreams are made.

In fields of white, the snowflakes glide,
A gentle dance, the world's great pride.
In every flake, a story told,
Drifting frost, a vision bold.

As sun ascends, the spell moves on,
Yet in our hearts, it lingers long.
A fleeting touch, a magic lost,
Drifting frost, we count the cost.

Jewel of the Pale Moon

In silvery glow, the night does gleam,
A orb of light, a whispered dream.
Beneath its watch, the shadows play,
Warriors of dusk, they drift away.

Soft as a sigh, the world does still,
With every breath, the heart does thrill.
The moon, a jewel in velvet skies,
Guides the lost with gentle eyes.

In quiet realms, where secrets dwell,
The pale moon casts a timeless spell.
A guardian of lovers' plight,
Forever shines, a beacon bright.

As night unfolds, the stories weave,
In silver light, our dreams believe.
A canvas vast, where wishes soar,
The pale moon whispers evermore.

So linger not in fading light,
Embrace the glow, the silent night.
For in its grasp, we come alive,
The jewel shines, where hearts revive.

Tapestry of Ice

Threads of frost, so finely spun,
Drape the land, a chill begun.
Each crystal forms a tale untold,
In frozen frames, the world unfolds.

Shimmering paths of gleaming white,
A fairy's brush, a dance of light.
In silver whispers, secrets shared,
The fabric speaks of dreams ensnared.

Branches bowed with frosted grace,
Nature's art, a perfect lace.
Icicles hang, like chandeliers,
Reflecting hopes, dissolving fears.

A world in slumber, hushed and still,
Awaits the warmth, a fiery thrill.
But in this pause, the beauty lies,
In every breath, the chill defies.

So walk with care on frozen ground,
Where beauty's song is softly found.
In tapestry of ice, we see,
A fleeting glimpse of harmony.

Shimmering Wintry Lace

Falling softly, the snowflakes dance,
In quiet moments, they take their chance.
A lace of white on earth's embrace,
Transforming all with delicate grace.

Windows gleam in cozy light,
As shadows weave with the fall of night.
A world wrapped tight in nature's shawl,
Each flake a whisper that gently calls.

Children's laughter fills the air,
As snowmen rise from winter's care.
Their joyous shouts break winter's spell,
In a kingdom where enchantments dwell.

The trees adorned in icy crowns,
Stand tall and proud, the silence drowns.
Each branch a story, each flake a dream,
In shimmering lace, a world supreme.

So let us pause, and take it in,
This wintry dance, where dreams begin.
Embrace the chill, the fleeting chance,
In shimmering lace, let spirits prance.

Veiled in Frost

Morning breaks, with icy breath,
A world transformed, a dance with death.
Veils of frost on fields do lay,
Nature's quiet, a soft display.

Across the glass, the sunlight creeps,
Awakening dreams from slumber deep.
The icy veil begins to fade,
Revealing life in twilight laid.

Whispers of winter, secrets told,
As nature's tapestry unfolds.
In frosty air, a crystal laugh,
Reflects the warmth of the sun's path.

Beneath the veil, life stirs anew,
In every branch, a vibrant hue.
The frost may bind, but can't contain,
The pulse of spring, the spark of rain.

So cherish moments, fleeting, bright,
In winter's grasp, find pure delight.
For in the frost, life's whispers hide,
A promise kept, as time does glide.

Glistening Veins

In the heart of the forest, whispers flow,
Silver streams weaving, a delicate show.
Underneath branches, where shadows play,
Glistening veins guide us, night turns to day.

Moonlight dances on leaves so bright,
Embers of stars spark the velvet night.
Nature's embrace, a soothing balm,
In the silence profound, we find our calm.

Among the roots where secrets lie,
Echoes of laughter, the softest sigh.
Alluring paths where dreams take flight,
Glistening veins shimmer, a wondrous sight.

Winds weave tales of ages past,
Through time and space, memories cast.
In every ripple, a story unfolds,
Glistening veins revealing what love holds.

So let us wander, hand in hand,
In nature's tapestry, forever we'll stand.
With hearts entwined beneath the fray,
Glistening veins guide our souls, come what may.

Ethereal Chill

In the hush of dawn, a whispering breeze,
Frosted petals shimmer, delicate as ease.
Veils of mist drift, secrets untold,
Ethereal chill wraps the world in cold.

Crystal facets dance on the frozen ground,
Nature's quiet sighs, a soft, eerie sound.
In this cool embrace, we find our way,
With each breath, we linger, and dare to stay.

Morning will break with a warm golden hue,
But in this stillness, the heart finds true.
Moments suspended, wrapped in time,
Ethereal chill, a rhythm, a rhyme.

Underneath star-kissed skies that glow,
Each silent heartbeat sets the pace slow.
In the clutches of winter's soft kiss,
Woven together, we find our bliss.

As daylight beckons with promises bright,
The chilling allure fades into the light.
Yet memories linger, in shadows they fill,
Forever enchanted by this ethereal chill.

Crystalized Dreams

In the depth of night, visions gleam,
Woven together, a fragile seam.
Sparkling wonders in a starlit stream,
Whispers of fortune in crystalized dreams.

Each thought a glimmer, lightly spun,
Beneath the silver, where wishes run.
Chasing reflections in the moon's silver beams,
Guided by fate through our crystalized dreams.

Moments suspended in a shimmering trance,
Glories of memories, a dance of chance.
Beauty enveloped in delicate themes,
Lost in the magic of crystalized dreams.

Winds carry secrets, a soft serenade,
Echoes of hope in the twilight cascade.
In this sweet slumber, nothing redeems,
Dreamers awaken to find their dreams.

Together we wander on stardust lanes,
Exploring forever where joy still reigns.
In the heart, a spark, love's guiding streams,
A life intertwined through crystalized dreams.

Frosted Serenity

In the still of night, peace softly falls,
Beneath frosted heavens, the silence calls.
Snowflakes flutter, a delicate ballet,
Frosted serenity grace the day.

Whispers of winter weave through the trees,
A tranquil embrace carried by the breeze.
With every breath, we find ways to sway,
In this quiet refuge, we choose to stay.

The world is hushed, wrapped in pure white,
Each flake a song, a moment so bright.
Gentle reflections, time moves astray,
In frosted serenity, dreams come to play.

Under the starlight, our hearts align,
Finding solace where shadows entwine.
Nature's soft cradle, where troubles decay,
In the calm of the night, we drift away.

As dawn awakens, painting the skies,
The beauty remains, woven in sighs.
In every silence, peace holds sway,
Forever embraced in frosted serenity's way.

Winter's Delicate Embrace

A blanket white, so pure and light,
It holds the world in softest sight.
Amidst the trees, the whispers soar,
As silence sings, and echoes bore.

The chill caress, a gentle breath,
In frozen moments, dances death.
Each flake that falls, a fleeting art,
Embraces all within its heart.

The world transformed, a canvas bright,
In winter's grasp, we find delight.
With every step, the crunch resounds,
In harmony, our joy abounds.

The sun retreats, the stars awake,
In frosty air, our dreams partake.
Each fleeting ray, a promise new,
As winter's spell brings forth the true.

Hand in hand, we wander far,
Underneath the glistening star.
In winter's arms, we finds our grace,
Forever in this warm embrace.

Crystal-Threaded Night

The night unfolds in threads of gleam,
Each star a song, a whispered dream.
The moonlight weaves a silver thread,
In twilight's dance, our fears are shed.

Soft breezes kiss the waking trees,
As shadows sway with gentle ease.
In crystal glow, the world will shine,
A tapestry, both yours and mine.

The stillness sings a calming tune,
Beneath the watchful, weary moon.
In moments held, the heart can soar,
In crystal night, we dream once more.

The heavens spill their jeweled light,
A canvas drawn on velvet night.
In every breath, a story spun,
As dreams ignite, and hearts are won.

Embrace the dark, for it holds grace,
In crystal-threaded night's embrace.
With every star, a tale unfolds,
In silken dreams, our fate beholds.

Silvery Frost

The dawn arrives in frosty breath,
A silvery sheen, a dance with death.
Each blade of grass, a frozen jewel,
In morning's light, the world is cool.

Across the field, the crystals gleam,
In nature's grasp, a soft daydream.
The air is still, as time holds fast,
In silvery frost, we find the past.

The trees adorned in icy lace,
Their branches curve in winter's grace.
With every step, a whispered sigh,
The frosted air, a gentle high.

The sun breaks through the chilly shroud,
As warmth returns, no longer proud.
Yet in the shade, the frost remains,
A memory of winter's chains.

In moments brief, we pause to see,
The beauty found in cold decree.
For silvery frost, both harsh and sweet,
In nature's hand, our hearts shall meet.

Luminous Shimmer

In twilight's glow, the shadows play,
The luminous shimmer leads the way.
Reflections dance on water's edge,
As dreams swirl softly, like a pledge.

With every glimmer, hope ignites,
A beacon bright in starry nights.
The whispered winds of ancient tales,
Weaving through the heart, it sails.

Each flicker speaks of time and fate,
A luminescent path, so great.
Beneath the stars, we wander free,
In every glimpse, our souls agree.

As dawn arrives, the shimmer fades,
Yet in our hearts, the light cascades.
Forever bound, by hope's embrace,
In luminous shimmer, we find our place.

Delicate Crystals

On branches bare, the crystals gleam,
A fleeting moment, like a dream.
Whispers of ice in the softest light,
Nature's art, a stunning sight.

Fragile forms, each one unique,
Silent beauty, words can't speak.
In the stillness, they dance and play,
A fleeting magic that fades away.

A breath of chill in the morning air,
Delicate wonders, beyond compare.
Caught in the dawn's embracing glow,
A world transformed, in sparkles flow.

Nature's canvas, painted bright,
Crystalline beauty, pure delight.
Capturing light in every crest,
In winter's grasp, they find their rest.

With every glance, a story told,
Of fleeting moments, bright and bold.
In the heart of winter's chill,
Delicate crystals, silent thrill.

Frosted Canopy

Beneath a sky of pastel hues,
A frosted canopy gently brews.
Branches draped in icy lace,
Nature's quilt, a tranquil space.

Softly falls the powdery snow,
Blanketing earth in a hushed glow.
As whispers of winter weave anew,
A frosted world in every view.

The trees stand tall, a sculpted art,
Coated in frost, they play their part.
In the stillness, magic brews,
Underneath the sky of blues.

Frozen whispers hang in the air,
A delicate touch that's oh so rare.
Each branch adorned, a graceful sight,
A frosted canopy, pure and bright.

As shadows dance in the fading light,
A symphony of cold in the night.
Nature pauses, holding its breath,
In the beauty of winter's depth.

Glimmering Hues of Cold

In the twilight, colors ignite,
Glimmering hues, a chilly sight.
Blues and purples swirl and blend,
A vivid canvas, without end.

Icicles hang like frozen dreams,
Reflecting light in silver beams.
A tapestry, woven by the frost,
Each moment cherished, never lost.

The world adorned in crystalline coats,
Nature's brush paints, as it floats.
Through the twilight, shadows creep,
In winter's grasp, the world is steep.

Underneath stars, the magic flows,
In glimmering hues, the quiet glows.
A dance of colors, crisp and bold,
A promise of warmth when winter's cold.

Each hue tells tales of frosty nights,
Of glimmering secrets, hidden sights.
A fleeting beauty, that can't be caught,
In glimmering hues, our spirits sought.

Midwinter's Breath

In the hush of the chilling air,
Midwinter's breath, a subtle flare.
Each exhale a whisper of dreams,
Transforming the world in silver beams.

Frosted breaths of trees so tall,
Nature's symphony, a gentle call.
In frozen stillness, hearts unite,
Beneath the stars, a tranquil night.

The moonlight dances on the snow,
A celestial warmth that starts to glow.
As shadows stretch and twilight fades,
Midwinter's breath in serenades.

Crystalline wonders catch our gaze,
In subtle beauty, we lose our ways.
Each moment wrapped in icy lace,
A tender touch, a warm embrace.

So let us breathe this magic in,
In midwinter's breath, new lives begin.
In every flake, a promise shines,
Of brighter days and warmer signs.

Flawless Chill

The winter air whispers soft,
Bare trees stand, bravely aloft.
Snowflakes dance in the pale light,
Wrapped in silence, the world feels right.

Footsteps crunch on frosty ground,
Laughter echoes, joy profound.
Breath hangs like clouds in the breeze,
Moments linger, hearts at ease.

Radiance in the soft white glow,
Every shadow glimmers slow.
Stars above, a twinkling quilt,
In this season, love is built.

Hot cocoa warms our hands tight,
As we gather, hearts ignite.
Underneath a blanket's fold,
Stories shared, memories unfold.

The perfect chill wraps around,
In this magic, we are found.
Together here, we dance and play,
Flawless winter, come what may.

Frosted Dreams

In the stillness of the night,
Moonbeams cast a silver light.
Underneath a frosted sky,
Dreams take flight and softly sigh.

Whispers woven in the air,
Frozen tales beyond compare.
Each breath visible, a puff,
In this world, winter is enough.

Stars like diamonds, cold yet bright,
Guide us gently through the night.
Time stands still, the world asleep,
In our hearts, the dreams we keep.

A journey across the land,
Hand in hand, we understand.
Frosted edges, kisses sweet,
In the silence, moments meet.

Wrapped in warmth, our spirits soar,
In this glimmer, we explore.
Frosted dreams beneath the dome,
In winter's heart, we find our home.

Veils of Winter Light

A tapestry of silver white,
Frosted branches catch the light.
Shadows linger, softly speak,
In this wonder, we feel weak.

Crystals twinkle, nature's grace,
In the chill, our hearts embrace.
Hushed, the world holds its breath tight,
Veils of beauty in the night.

Steps adorned in glimmering snow,
Every path a story to know.
Under stars, secrets flow,
In the stillness, time moves slow.

Cascading flakes from skies above,
Wrap the earth in gentle love.
Harmony sings through frozen air,
A winter's veil, a whispered prayer.

Here we stand, the moment's glow,
In this magic, we let go.
Veils of winter, softly spun,
Together, our hearts are one.

Enchanted Ice

A world transformed by icy breath,
Whispers linger, thoughts of death.
Yet in the chill, there's magic bright,
In every corner, pure delight.

Frosty patterns grace each pane,
Nature's artwork, splendid gain.
With every step, the echoes call,
Enchanted ice surrounds us all.

Footprints leave a tale untold,
Memories wrapped in shades of gold.
In this realm where dreams conspire,
Hearts ignite, our spirits fire.

Crystal castles rise and sway,
Underneath the moon's soft play.
Every moment feels so grand,
Enchantment lies within our hands.

Breathe in deep, the frosty air,
Feel the magic everywhere.
In the chill, our laughter sings,
Enchanted ice, the joy it brings.

Fragile Beauty

In a world of fleeting grace,
Petals fall, a soft embrace.
Colors fade, yet still they glow,
Whispers of a time we know.

Tender moments ever bright,
Captured in the fading light.
Hold them close, let them stay,
Fragile beauty leads the way.

Like a dream that dances low,
In the wind, where secrets flow.
Yet they leave their mark so clear,
Memories we hold so dear.

Time will weave its gentle thread,
Through the heart where hope is fed.
Even as we try to keep,
Fragile beauty starts to sleep.

In our hearts, it finds a home,
In our souls, it likes to roam.
Though it's fleeting, it is true,
Fragile beauty lives in you.

Silver Thread Through Silence

In the hush of twilight's grace,
Whispers dance in soft embrace.
Stars are stitched in velvet skies,
Woven tales, where silence lies.

Moonlight glimmers on the dew,
Threads of silver, fresh and new.
Nature holds her breath in awe,
Every moment bound by law.

Softly, night begins to weave,
Dreams that gently interleave.
Every shadow tells a tale,
Marching forth like ghostly sail.

Echoed hearts start to align,
Time unwinds like spun design.
In the stillness, we can find,
Silver thread in silence twined.

Through the dark, we catch a glimpse,
Of the magic that it hints.
Hopeful hearts and quiet sighs,
Silver threads that light the skies.

Natures Glassy Cascade

Water flows with gentle grace,
Nature's glassy, pure embrace.
Over stones, it sings and sighs,
Reflecting dreams in azure skies.

Dancing lightly, free and bold,
Stories of the earth retold.
Every droplet speaks a name,
Echoing the wild's sweet fame.

In the sunlight, sparkles play,
Turning moments into day.
Cascading down, it finds its way,
Nature's voice in soft array.

Beneath the trees, the waters gleam,
Whispers caught in nature's dream.
In the rush, we feel it call,
Life's own rhythm, one and all.

Flowing on, forever grand,
In its course, we understand.
In this world, so wild and free,
Natures glassy cascade be.

Whispering Winter

Snowflakes dance on chilly air,
Carrying secrets everywhere.
Whispers soft as shadows blend,
Nature's breath, a gentle friend.

Frosted branches, quiet grace,
Each a tale in this white space.
Winter wraps the world in dreams,
Silence flows in silver streams.

Through the stillness, whispers rise,
Beneath the cold and starry skies.
Every heart feels winter's kiss,
Silent nights that bring us bliss.

In the snow, footprints trace,
Stories shared in winter's face.
Huddled close, we find our way,
In this world where cold may play.

Whispering winter, calm and bright,
Holds the flame of shared delight.
In the chill, we're not alone,
In the warmth, our love is grown.

Diamond Threads of Dawn

The sun breaks softly on the hill,
Each ray a thread, a warming thrill.
In hues of gold, the morning sings,
Awakening dreams, unfurling wings.

The sky adorned in shades so bright,
Promises dance in the morning light.
With every breath, the world feels new,
A canvas fresh, in every hue.

Birds take flight on whispered breeze,
Nature's chorus, a joyful tease.
Each note a promise, pure and free,
Of daybreak's hope, of what could be.

Whispers of dew on blades of grass,
In silence, moments slip and pass.
Yet in this hour, the heart can bind,
To life's sweet song, to dreams unwind.

As day unfolds, embrace the glow,
With diamond threads that softly flow.
In every dawn, a chance bestowed,
To weave our tales on morning's road.

Ensnared by the Cold

Whispers of winter haunt the air,
A chill that lingers, stark and rare.
The world draped in a frosty veil,
As shadows stretch and soft winds wail.

Each breath a mist, a fleeting dance,
In silence, hearts caught in a trance.
The trees stand still, their branches bare,
Guardians of secrets, held with care.

Footsteps crunch on a bed of snow,
Where silence reigns, and cold winds blow.
The moon casts beams on the frozen land,
A silvery touch, a gentle hand.

Stars twinkle down from a canvas dark,
Each one a whisper, each one a spark.
Embrace the night, the winter's breath,
In shadows deep, find beauty's depth.

Yet in this frigid, hushed embrace,
Lies warmth within, a tender grace.
For even cold holds stories old,
Of warmth beneath, in hearts we hold.

Serenity's Crystal Wisp

In fleeting moments, whispers bloom,
Soft as the light in a quiet room.
A crystal wisp, so pure and bright,
Guides the soul through gentle night.

The world slows down, as time suspends,
In tranquil spaces, where stillness blends.
Each heartbeat echoes, calm and clear,
In serenity's glow, all is near.

The stars above in quiet gleam,
Reflect the hopes of a secret dream.
With every sigh, the mind can roam,
In crystal light, we find our home.

Nature whispers in a soft caress,
Inviting hearts to find their rest.
In every shadow, peace is found,
As moments linger, joy unbound.

So let the silence weave its spell,
In gentle whispers, all will dwell.
A crystal wisp, through night we glide,
In serenity's embrace, we bide.

The Art of Silent Winters

In stillness wrapped, as dusk descends,
The art of winter, where silence mends.
Each flake a brushstroke, soft and white,
Painting the world in the cloak of night.

Frost-kissed trees, in grandeur stand,
Guardians of time, they understand.
With whispers low, they keep their tales,
Of icy winds and gentle gales.

Hushed are the echoes of footfalls near,
In winter's hold, all feels sincere.
The moonlight spills on a canvas pure,
A silent promise, quiet and sure.

Embrace the cold, the tranquil charm,
In each moment, find the warm.
For in this art, in silent nights,
Lies a beauty that ignites.

So pause and breathe in the crisp, clear air,
In winter's embrace, there's magic rare.
The art of silent winters unfolds,
In stories whispered, in wonders told.

Chilling Serenity

In the quiet of the night,
Whispers dance with cold delight.
Stars blink softly far away,
While shadows weave in moonlit play.

Breath of frost on frozen ground,
A world where peace can be found.
Frosted branches sway and bow,
Nature holds its breath, and how.

Crickets sing their final song,
While night stretches deep and long.
The air is crisp, the sky is wide,
In this moment, all abide.

Dew drops glimmer like lost dreams,
Caught within the silver beams.
The heart is still, the mind is clear,
Chilling serenity draws near.

Wrapped in silence, pure and deep,
Into the night, the soul will seep.
Each heartbeat matches nature's tone,
In the chill, we find our home.

Twisted Mirrors of January

Frosted windows, figures blur,
In hazy mirrors, thoughts concur.
January holds a chilling breath,
Reflecting life in whispered death.

Footsteps crunch on icy trails,
Echoes tell of winter's tales.
Frosty fingers trace the glass,
Twisted futures yet to pass.

The world feels different, turned around,
In mirrored reflections, lost is found.
Shadows cross paths, intertwine,
In January's grasp, we redefine.

Silence reigns in tranquil frost,
Each moment cherished, never lost.
Nature's canvas, stark and bare,
In the cold, we find our share.

In twisted mirrors, truth decays,
Life replays in muted phase.
Through icy lenses, dreams unfold,
January's grip, both harsh and bold.

Lunar Icework

Underneath the silver moon,
Icework shimmers, night's soft tune.
Crystals dance in gentle light,
Holding secrets close and tight.

Frozen rivers weave and glide,
Nature's magic, pure and wide.
The stillness breathes a quiet song,
In lunar glow, we drift along.

Stars adorn the midnight sky,
Bright reflections, echo sighs.
Whispers of the night breeze play,
Guiding dreams that drift away.

A canvas painted in the dark,
With every shadow, a little spark.
In this icework, hearts unite,
Beneath the watchful, luminous light.

As clouds drift softly, shadows weave,
In lunar embrace, we believe.
Moments captured, time so still,
In the moon's glow, hearts we fill.

Silvery Graces

Delicate patterns fall like lace,
In the air, I sense their grace.
Snowflakes spinning, soft and slow,
Each a story yet to show.

Underneath the winter's hush,
Nature breathes, a gentle rush.
Frozen whispers fill the night,
Bathed in pure, enchanting light.

Trees stand clothed in silver dreams,
Basked in moonlight's glowing beams.
Every branch, with beauty graced,
In this moment, time is chased.

Warmth of hearts in cold embrace,
Silvery laughter takes its place.
In each flake, a wish, a prayer,
Frosted wonders fill the air.

When morning comes, reflections gleam,
In the light, we find our theme.
Silvery graces, soft and bright,
Illuminate the wintry night.

Shards of Serenity

In quiet whispers, shadows play,
Fragments of peace chase night away.
Softly they glimmer, secrets unfold,
Stories of silence, softly told.

A tapestry woven with threads of grace,
Moments reflecting a tranquil space.
Each shard a memory, shining bright,
Guiding the heart through the still of the night.

Beneath the starry, vast expanse,
Nature beckons in a gentle dance.
Waves of calm like a soothing tide,
In the realm of solace, we abide.

With every breath, a new dawn wakes,
Awakening dreams, the heart remakes.
Shards of serenity, pearls divine,
Echoes of love in every line.

Each fragment holds a silent prayer,
Whispers of hope in the cool night air.
Together they shimmer, together they glow,
In the stillness, beauty does flow.

Glacial Veils

Amidst the frost, a veiled disguise,
Earth dressed in crystals, a sight so wise.
Whispers of winter in shimmering white,
As nature unfolds her delicate light.

Frozen rivers rush with quiet grace,
Reflecting the azure of the sky's embrace.
Glacial veils drape the ancient trees,
A masterpiece born from the breeze.

Each flake a story, a breath of the cold,
In delicate patterns, the night unfolds.
Under the moon's watchful gaze,
The landscape dances in frozen haze.

Gentle murmur of snowy sighs,
Under a canvas where magic lies.
Time slows down in winter's hold,
Moments captured, a charm untold.

Between the branches, light filters through,
A story of winter, pure and true.
Glacial veils, a wonderland's call,
In the heart of the frost, we find it all.

Enchanted Chill

In the breath of night, a magic stirs,
Caressed by a chill, the world occurs.
Stars twinkle softly in the velvet deep,
While secrets of silence ever so creep.

Moonlit shadows dance upon the ground,
With every heartbeat, enchantment is found.
The air hangs heavy with dreams untold,
Wrapped in the rhythm of nature's fold.

Embers of warmth flicker and fade,
The chill of the night, a soft serenade.
Awakening frost on windowpanes,
Whispers of winter with gentle refrains.

In the stillness, hearts find their way,
Holding the magic of night and day.
An enchanted chill, a fleeting embrace,
Where moments linger, lost in space.

Each breath of air, crisp and clear,
Under the spell of the atmosphere.
With every shiver, wonder grows,
In the enchanted chill, life softly flows.

Twinkling Frostwork

Under the blanket of silvery night,
Frostwork glistens, a delicate sight.
Each tiny crystal, a star set free,
In the still of the air, a symphony.

Patterns emerge, intricate and fine,
Nature's artistry in every line.
Twinkling frostwork, a fleeting art,
Capturing magic that warms the heart.

Gentle caress of the winter's breath,
Painting the world with a touch of death.
Yet in the stillness, life takes a stand,
Under the spell of a frozen hand.

Beneath the moon, shadows dance and play,
Frosted whispers guide the way.
Every glimmer a story to tell,
Of winter's charm, spellbinding and swell.

As daylight breaks, the crystals will fade,
But memories linger, never to trade.
Twinkling frostwork, a dreamer's delight,
In the heart of winter, pure and bright.

Sparkling Enigma

In shadows deep, a glint does play,
Mysterious lights in disarray.
Whispers of truth in silence swirl,
A puzzle wrapped in a shimmering pearl.

Glimmers tease the weary mind,
A riddle lost, yet fate entwined.
Through tangled thoughts, the spark ignites,
Illuminating the darkest nights.

Each flicker hints at dreams concealed,
The heart's desires gently revealed.
A dance of light, a fleeting chance,
To step beyond the mundane dance.

Mystique lingered in every gleam,
Awakening each forgotten dream.
In every spark, a story spun,
A never-ending race begun.

At journey's end, will we behold,
The secrets scattered, mysteries sold?
In every enigma, beauty lies,
A spark that brightens the darkest skies.

Natures Frosted Artistry

On winter's breath, the crystals form,
A world transformed, a painted norm.
Snowflakes dance on the brisk, cold air,
Each one unique, beyond compare.

Trees don coats of shimmering white,
Nature's canvas, a pure delight.
Icicles hang with a graceful flair,
Glistening jewels in the frosty glare.

The sun peeks through, cast in gold,
Painting the scene in hues bold.
Branches bow under winter's weight,
While silence reigns, a tranquil state.

Footprints mark the untouched ground,
In solitude, nature's sound.
Every breath a cloud, so light,
A fleeting moment, pure and bright.

In twilight's glow, the world holds still,
With frosted beauty, a heart to fill.
Nature's artistry, a timeless grace,
In winter's arms, we find our place.

Shimmering Isolation

In a world of whispers, silence glows,
A shimmering presence nobody knows.
Beneath the stars, in shadows cast,
Loneliness wraps like a shroud amassed.

Gentle breezes hum a soft tune,
While shadows waltz beneath the moon.
In quiet corners where secrets form,
Isolation blooms, vibrant, warm.

Echoes linger in empty halls,
A rare beauty in silence calls.
Moments cherished in solitude's grace,
Finding solace in the empty space.

Reflection dances in fading light,
Revealing truths hidden from sight.
In the stillness, a heart exposed,
Shimmering bright, yet enclosed.

Embracing the peace of one's own view,
In isolation, find something true.
For in the quiet, mysteries grow,
A shimmering depth only we know.

Glacial Grace

Frozen rivers carve the earth's face,
Nature's art, pure glacial grace.
Mountains rise in majestic form,
Whispers of ice, a silent storm.

Snow-draped valleys breathe softly bright,
Underneath the soft moonlight.
Glaciers creeping, ancient and wise,
A timeless dance beneath the skies.

Whispers of ages in splintered ice,
Nature's legacy, cold but nice.
In every crack, a story lies,
Of epochs gone, where silence flies.

The air grows thin as time stands still,
In frozen dreams, a bitter chill.
Yet in this expanse, beauty reigns,
As glacial grace forever remains.

In winter's hush, we find our peace,
Amidst the stillness, worries cease.
In glacial realms, we come to see,
The elegant truth of serenity.

Enchanted Suspension

In the heart of the forest, silence sings,
Whispers of magic in winter's wings.
Branches adorned with crystalline lace,
Nature's own treasure, a frozen embrace.

Moonlight weaves through the spectral trees,
Casting a spell with the gentlest breeze.
Each shadow dances, a ghostly ballet,
The night wears a cloak of shimmering gray.

Time seems to linger, a beautiful pause,
Enchanting the world without any cause.
Stars twinkle softly in the ink-black sky,
A picturesque realm where dreams seem to fly.

Footsteps muffled on powdery snow,
Where the secrets of winter begin to show.
A soft breath of frost, a delicate sigh,
Life's enchanted moments that never say goodbye.

Awakening whispers in the stillness of night,
Crafting illusions that feel just right.
In this enchanted realm, all fears take flight,
Suspended in magic, beneath the moonlight.

Frost's Caress

Gentle fingers of frost touch the ground,
Creating a beauty that knows no bound.
Nature wrapped in a glistening sheet,
A crystal carpet beneath our feet.

Each blade of grass, a frozen gem,
Morning sun kisses, a subtle hymn.
Nature's breath captured, a delicate art,
Frost's gentle caress warms the cold heart.

Icicles hanging, a fairy's delight,
Dripping in rhythm, reflecting the light.
Whispers of winter fill the crisp air,
In this frosty realm, there's magic to share.

Under the trees, in shadows they dwell,
Stories of old that our hearts can tell.
A world made anew in shimmering white,
Frost's caress dances in morning's light.

As dusk falls softly, bids the day adieu,
Each breath freezes, a moment so true.
Embraced by the chill, we find warmth in our souls,
In frost's gentle hold, our spirit unrolls.

Winter's Tender Veil

Wrapped in white, the world feels new,
Winter's gentle arms cradle the blue.
Snowflakes whisper a lullaby sweet,
Nature sleeps softly, its heartbeat discreet.

A tender veil drapes over the land,
Muffled echoes where once we stood grand.
Frozen rivers, a tranquil expanse,
Inviting us all to a magical dance.

Footprints are stories left in the frost,
Memories shimmer where warmth is lost.
Under the stars, the night softly glows,
Winter's tender touch forever bestows.

The air holds secrets, a chill in our bones,
Yet deep in this stillness, we're never alone.
As the moonlight bathes the snowflakes above,
We find in this quiet, the whispers of love.

So embrace this season with open hearts wide,
For winter's tender veil is a lullaby's guide.
In each crystal flake that dances and swirls,
We discover the magic that swathes our worlds.

Shimmering Illusion

In the twilight glow of a frost-kissed dream,
Illusions shimmer, a delicate gleam.
Stars caught in branches weave stories untold,
A tapestry of winter, both soft and bold.

Mirrors of ice reflect the night's song,
Dancing with shadows, where whispers belong.
Each flake a secret, a story of old,
Shimmering tales that the night has enfolded.

The moon casts a glow, a silver embrace,
Guiding the wanderers through time and space.
In this realm of magic, reality bends,
Where dreams blend with truth, and the journey ascends.

In the hush of the night, the world holds its breath,
As nature unveils her beauty in depth.
Within this illusion, we wander and roam,
Finding solace and magic, a world we call home.

So let us chase dreams in this glimmering glow,
Through shimmering illusions where wild spirits flow.
With hearts wide open, we dance in delight,
Embracing the magic, our souls take flight.

Winter's Silk

Softly falls the snow at night,
Blankets wrapped in purest white.
Whispers dance on frosty breeze,
Nature sighs, a quiet tease.

Branches bend with icy lace,
Silent woods, a tranquil space.
Moonlight glimmers, gentle glow,
Winter's silk, a magic show.

Footprints mark the silent ground,
In the stillness, peace is found.
Stars above like diamonds bright,
Winter's charm, a true delight.

Hot cocoa warms both hand and heart,
From the cold, we drift apart.
Gather close, let stories flow,
As the world turns soft and slow.

Fires crackle, shadows play,
In our hearts, the warmth will stay.
Embrace the chill, let worries cease,
Winter's silk brings us peace.

Frigid Flurries

Frigid flurries swirl and dance,
In the air, a fleeting chance.
Children laugh, they spin and twirl,
Nature's spark, a winter swirl.

Frosty breath in morning light,
Winter's grip, a pure delight.
Snowflakes kiss the frozen earth,
Blanketing the world in mirth.

Crisp and clear, the air so bright,
Every tree adorned in white.
Sleds come racing down the hill,
Joyful hearts, they laugh and thrill.

Icicles hang like crystal tears,
Chilling winds ride on our fears.
Yet within, warmth will ignite,
Frigid flurries feel just right.

Evening falls, the stars appear,
A frozen world, so crystal clear.
In the quiet, dreams take flight,
Frigid flurries, purest white.

Chilling Graces

Chilling graces in the air,
Whispers soft, beyond compare.
Nature holds her breath in time,
Winter's song, a gentle rhyme.

Frosty patterns on the glass,
Moments slip away too fast.
Quiet nights, the world at peace,
In winter's grasp, we find release.

Snowflakes dance like tiny lights,
Filling dark with purest whites.
Every branch a masterpiece,
Chilling graces bring us peace.

Frozen lakes reflect the sky,
Nature's mirror, oh so shy.
Hear the world's soft, whispered song,
In this stillness, we belong.

As the sunset paints the night,
Hearts aglow with warm delight.
Within the cold, a fire burns,
Chilling graces, joy returns.

Pearlescent Hues

Pearlescent hues adorn the dawn,
Winter's canvas, crisp and drawn.
Every shade a tale untold,
Nature's beauty, pure and bold.

Gentle blush of morning mist,
Soft and warm, a lover's kiss.
As the sun begins to rise,
Painted skies, a sweet surprise.

Snowflakes shimmer, diamonds rare,
Cascading down with tender care.
In the light, they sparkle free,
Pearlescent hues enchantingly.

Branches glisten, icy jewels,
Spectrums dance, as nature rules.
Fields aglow with morning's grace,
Every corner finds its place.

In this realm of softest white,
Hearts are lifted, spirits light.
As we wander, side by side,
Pearlescent hues, our joy and pride.

Sub-zero Anthems

In the hush of winter's breath,
Notes of ice weave through the trees,
Silent echoes linger here,
Chilling wind sings soft decrees.

Glittering on frozen ground,
Footprints trace a brittle song,
Melodies of solitude,
Where the frosty shadows throng.

Beneath a sky of crystal stars,
Whispers weave in silver threads,
Harmonies of the night air,
Dance where cold and silence spread.

Each flake falls like whispered notes,
Filling voids with icy grace,
Nature's orchestra unfolds,
In this frigid, tranquil space.

Sub-zero dreams are born anew,
Frosted visions in the night,
With each breath, a fleeting tune,
In the cold's embrace, we write.

Icy Embroidery

Threads of white in snowy lace,
Stitching patterns pure and fine,
Nature's artistry displayed,
In the winter's chill divine.

Every flake a tiny tale,
Crafted by the frosty breath,
Woven in the night so pale,
Imprints of a whispered death.

Branches draped in diamond dust,
Ornate designs across the land,
Sparkling under moon's soft gaze,
A tale only ice can stand.

In the stillness, beauty grows,
Enfolded in the quiet night,
Heavens weave their frigid threads,
Creating dreams of frosty light.

Icy tales with every gust,
Embroidery of winter's might,
Each stitch holds a frozen wish,
Crafting magic in the night.

Frosty Elegance

Glistening blooms in a frosty world,
Petals of silver, soft and bright,
Elegance in cold attire,
Whispers of beauty in the night.

The grace of winter's loving hand,
Caressing earth with tender care,
Each breath a whisper, soft and grand,
Delectable dreams ride in the air.

Timeless charm in icy bounds,
Each moment still, yet ever flows,
Frosted jewels on nature's crown,
In every flake, a story grows.

Beneath the moon's enchanting glow,
The elegance of night awakes,
Drawing hearts to dance and sway,
As the frigid air gently shakes.

In the silence, beauty sings,
With frosty elegance all around,
We find a warmth in icy reigns,
In the cold's embrace, love is found.

Prismatic Chill

Colors dance in winter's breath,
Spectrum woven in the ice,
Rainbows hidden in the frost,
Nature's art, both rare and nice.

Prismatic lights in frozen lands,
Each hue a memory of light,
Beauty trapped in winter's hands,
Brightening the starry night.

Glistening crystals, secrets shared,
Their facets holding stories bold,
In the chill, creation stirred,
With radiant colors to behold.

Every snowflake tells a tale,
Of sunlit days and starry nights,
Rainbow dreams in a crystal veil,
Awakened by the moon's soft lights.

The prismatic chill embraces all,
Whispering secrets on the breeze,
In frozen splendor, we enthrall,
Embracing winter's wondrous freeze.

Celestial Frost

In the silence of night, stars align,
Whispers of frost dance, soft and divine.
Each breath of winter glimmers bright,
Hushed in the magic of silver light.

Crystals form on leaves with grace,
Nature's canvas, a tranquil space.
Under the moon, the world glows pale,
An ethereal beauty in each tale.

Branches wear coats of sparkling white,
A frosty wonderland, pure delight.
Footsteps crunch on the frozen ground,
Echoes of stillness, a peace profound.

With every sigh, the cold air bites,
Yet hearts are warmed by twinkling lights.
Celestial frost, a fleeting dream,
In this enchanted winter theme.

So let us gather, hand in hand,
And cherish this cold, fair, frosty land.
For in the chill, we find our cheer,
Embracing magic that lingers near.

Ethereal Crystals

Glisten like stars in the frozen sea,
Ethereal crystals, wild and free.
Each shard catches light, a spectrum bright,
In the quiet embrace of the night.

Frosted petals, a delicate bite,
Softly they shimmer in moon's pure light.
A chorus of sparkles, nature's own song,
Whispers of beauty, where hearts belong.

In winter's grasp, the world feels small,
Yet in its wonder, we feel it all.
A tapestry woven from cold and grace,
Time stands still in this sacred space.

Crystals tease with their glimmering hue,
Reflecting the dreams that we once knew.
Each frosty breath, a moment to hold,
Stories of winter in whispers told.

So let us wander through this bright maze,
Where crystals twinkle in frozen haze.
In this ethereal realm, we roam,
Finding our way, forever our home.

Glacial Curtain

Behind the glacial curtain, worlds concealed,
Mysteries whisper, truths revealed.
Chill of the breeze tells tales untold,
In realms of ice, where dreams unfold.

Icicles hanging like spears of glass,
Time flows slowly as moments pass.
A shimmering veil, blue and bright,
Cloaked in nature's breath, pure light.

Frost-kissed dreams wrapped in a shroud,
In quietude, the heart feels proud.
Each flake a wish, softly it falls,
Echoing silence in winter's halls.

Glacial mysteries, ancient and deep,
In the stillness, the world's secrets keep.
With every step, the earth feels alive,
In the cold embrace where hopes can thrive.

So let us venture beyond the ice,
Past the curtain where wonders entice.
In glacial beauty, we find our place,
In a world bathed in frost's gentle grace.

Frostbound Elegance

Frostbound elegance paints the dawn,
A delicate beauty, like a fawn.
Whispers of winter in every tree,
Nature's art, wild and free.

Velvet skies and a sun so low,
Crystals sparkle in the early glow.
A tapestry woven in white and gray,
Where dreams of chills and warmth sway.

In the hush of the morn, the world awakes,
Frosted lace on the shimmering lakes.
Beneath the layers, life persists,
In frostbound elegance, see the mist.

Glimmers of silver on branches spread,
Dancing softly where angels tread.
With each heartbeat, the cold air sings,
In serene moments, the warmth it brings.

So hold this beauty, let it unfold,
Frostbound tales in whispers told.
For in the stillness, we find our way,
Elegance lingers, brightening day.

Crystaline Tapestry

Threads of ice, a woven dream,
Glistening bright in the soft moonbeam.
Each shard reflects a story untold,
In the silence, magic unfolds.

Beneath the stars, a canvas fair,
Captured whispers dance in the air.
Fractals shimmer, colors collide,
A tapestry born where secrets abide.

Glimmers of crystal, spirits collide,
Echoes of nature, with grace, they glide.
Each sparkle, a moment held tight,
In the luminous tapestry of night.

Winds weave softly, a delicate sound,
In this realm, serenity found.
Nature's touch in every thread spun,
A crystalline world where all is one.

Here in stillness, beauty resides,
In a tapestry where wonder abides.
Moments captured, forever to last,
In the crystaline dance of the past.

Nature's Glass

Reflecting beams of sunlight's grace,
Each droplet shows a wondrous place.
Leaves adorned with glistening tears,
Life's vibrant pulse throughout the years.

Gentle streams that sing and flow,
Mirrored landscapes put on a show.
Through nature's glass, the world awakes,
In every shimmer, a heartbeat breaks.

Petals dance in an emerald hue,
Nature's beauty, forever anew.
Raindrops fall and diamonds form,
A liquid world, so soft and warm.

Mountains rise in radiant light,
Kissed by the dawn, a breathtaking sight.
In quiet moments, the heart can see,
The glass of nature, pure harmony.

Every glance, a fleeting kiss,
In this reflection, all is bliss.
Nature's glass, where dreams arise,
In sparkling wonders under the skies.

Whispered Frost

Quiet nights wrapped in icy breath,
Whispers of frost conjure up death.
Yet in the cold, a warmth remains,
A vibrant pulse where life sustains.

Frozen patterns etched in glass,
Each intricate line a fleeting pass.
Under moonlight's gentle caress,
Winter tells tales, soft and less.

Branches adorned in silver lace,
In the stillness, we embrace space.
Nature's secrets, breath of the cold,
In whispered frost, stories unfold.

The world slumbers beneath its white,
In the dark, dreams take flight.
With every flake, a dance begins,
Whispered frost, where silence spins.

When dawn appears, the glimmers fade,
Yet in our hearts, the beauty stayed.
In frosted whispers, moments throng,
In winter's grace, we all belong.

Shards of Dusk

As daylight wanes, colors ignite,
Scarlet skies succumb to night.
Shards of dusk, a fleeting sight,
Embrace the shadows, breathe in light.

Beneath the veil of twilight's hue,
The world transforms, alive and new.
Stars awaken, softly blink,
In this hour, we pause and think.

Whispers echo through the trees,
A gentle rustle from the breeze.
Nighttime dances on golden dreams,
In every corner, magic beams.

On the horizon, the sun retreats,
Painting skies where darkness meets.
In shards of dusk, the heart ignites,
In the stillness, a thousand Lights.

Embrace the night, let worries float,
In shadows deep, our hopes can coat.
For every dusk that comes to pass,
Is a promise born in night's vast glass.

Luminous Cold

Beneath the silver moon's embrace,
Whispers dance in icy air.
Stars are etched, a fleeting trace,
In the stillness, magic's rare.

Snowflakes twirl like dreams untold,
Crystals glimmer, softly break.
Nature's breath, a touch so bold,
In silence, hearts awake.

Frosted branches hold their sighs,
Each shimmer, a secret kept.
In the night where beauty lies,
Luminous, where cold is swept.

Echoes linger on the breeze,
Time stands still in midnight's glow.
Wrapped in wonder, softly freeze,
In this realm of ice and flow.

Cold unfolds a gentle art,
Painting white on earth and sky.
With each breath, we tear apart,
The darkness; here, we dare fly.

Glinting Fronds

In the breeze, the fronds do sway,
Sinister shadows, bright and bold.
Dewdrops glisten in the day,
Nature's jewels, green and gold.

Beneath the sun, they catch the light,
A dance of colors on display.
Whispers soft as day takes flight,
In a world where dreams hold sway.

Every curve a tale unwinds,
Of summer's warmth and gentle rain.
In their grace, a peace one finds,
Glinting fronds, they soothe the pain.

Roots entangled, life's embrace,
A tapestry of green and hue.
In their presence, time finds space,
To breathe anew, to start anew.

Listen closely to the song,
Of the fronds that sway and bend.
In their rhythm, we belong,
Glinting echoes, nature's friend.

Frosted Tresses

Whispers wrapped in winter's lace,
Frosted tresses, soft and mild.
Nature's brush, an artful grace,
Every strand, a story filed.

On the ground, a crystal quilt,
Glistening, a fleeting dream.
In the hush, a beauty built,
Frosted whispers in the gleam.

Underneath the barren trees,
Tresses twine in silent song.
Nature's breath, a gentle tease,
In this magic, we belong.

Fields of silver, pure and bright,
Embrace the dawn with open arms.
In the glow of morning light,
Frosted tresses weave their charms.

In their shimmer, moments freeze,
Capturing time in crystal frames.
In this world, we find our peace,
Frosted tresses call our names.

Gelid Silhouettes

Among the trees, the shadows creep,
   Gelid silhouettes take flight.
Forms that linger, softly seep,
   Into the fabric of the night.

Drifting softly through the dark,
   Whispers echo on the breeze.
In their depths, a hidden spark,
Shape of dreams beneath the trees.

In the frost, they sway and twist,
   Figures wrapped in icy grace.
In the silence, truths exist,
Veiled in shadows, time's embrace.

Every curve a fleeting ghost,
   Gelid outlines in the moon.
A spectral beauty, we can boast,
   In this night's quiet rune.

As dawn breaks, they fade away,
   Leaving echoes in their wake.
In the light, we start to play,
   Gelid silhouettes, hearts awake.

A Frosted Tangle

In the hush of dawn's soft light,
Frosted branches reach for the sky.
A tangle of white, pure and bright,
Nature's artistry, soaring high.

Beneath the weight of crystal dreams,
A world enchained, a silent plea.
Frosted whispers, gentle beams,
Nature's touch on every tree.

Glistening webs of icy lace,
Twining paths of frost and dew.
In every corner, a frozen grace,
A moment captured, fresh and new.

Frosted whispers in the air,
Secrets told in shaded glens.
A chilly calm, a breath of prayer,
In quiet turns, the stillness mends.

As winter's chill draws near and wide,
A frosted tangle, wild and free.
In nature's hold, we can abide,
In every breath, eternity.

Crystal Drapery

A veil of ice on softest boughs,
The world adorned in silver sheen.
Each branch a promise, nature sows,
A drapery crisp, a timeless scene.

The morning sun breaks, gently glows,
Reflecting gems on winter's bed.
Around the trees where cold wind blows,
A whispering chill, a dream unsaid.

With every step, the earth does sing,
Crystals crunch beneath our feet.
Nature's charm, an endless spring,
In frozen hues, our hearts skip beat.

Soft colors blend in evening's sigh,
Lavender, sapphire, deepening gray.
A canvas where the shadows lie,
In crystal drapery, night holds sway.

Each frosted petal, a story spun,
As starlight dances on the snow.
In winter's heart, we find our fun,
In crystal beauty, we shall glow.

Frozen Whispers

In the quiet of the night,
Frozen whispers start to play.
Voices carried by the light,
In the frost, they weave and sway.

The moon drapes silver on the ground,
Shadows flicker, thoughts take flight.
Every rustle, every sound,
Tells the tales of winter's night.

A breath of stories in the air,
Whispers linger, soft and clear.
In the stillness, dreams declare,
A frosty realm, no hint of fear.

With every step, the secrets flow,
Through glades where frost has kissed the leaf.
In frozen paths, we come to know,
The quiet grace of winter's brief.

As dawn awakes, the whispers fade,
Yet in our hearts, they leave a trace.
In frozen realms, our hopes are laid,
In whispered dreams, we find our place.

Shimmering Shards

Look upon the world, aglow,
With shimmering shards of ice and light.
Dance of prisms, subtle show,
Every angle, pure delight.

In the path of winter's chill,
Glistening crystals line the way.
A fleeting moment, time does still,
Shards of beauty, where dreams play.

Beneath a sky of tinted hue,
The world refracts in colors bright.
Every glance reveals anew,
The magic held in winter's night.

Light cascades in gentle streams,
Through branches draped in frosted lace.
Each fragment gleams with whispered dreams,
In shimmering shards, we find our grace.

As the sun begins to rise again,
The glowing shards give way to morn.
Yet every glimmer, every stain,
Holds a promise of day reborn.

Glacial Poetry

Amidst the ice, the silence sings,
A world wrapped tight in frosty rings.
Reflections dance on crystal blue,
Where every breath feels fresh and new.

Whispers echo through the snow,
Nature's art, a quiet glow.
Each flake a story, old yet bright,
Creating magic in the night.

The mountains stand with regal grace,
Embraced by winter's cold embrace.
Their peaks adorned with shining crowns,
Guardians of the frozen towns.

By rivers' edge, the stillness reigns,
As time moves slow, it softly gains.
The chill infuses every breath,
In glacial peace, there's no such death.

A tapestry of white and blue,
Beneath a sky of endless hue.
In every corner, beauty glows,
As glacial poetry gently flows.

Elegant Frostwork

Artistry in every inch,
Delicate patterns, nature's cinch.
Frosted branches, lace-like threads,
Whispers of winter where beauty spreads.

Each morning brings a crystal dawn,
As sunlight kisses the frozen lawn.
A moment's peace, a breath so rare,
In the shimmer of the frosty air.

Trees adorned like regal queens,
In flowing gowns of icy sheens.
Branches bow with elegant grace,
A frozen world, a slow embrace.

The chill enchants the quiet skies,
Transforming earth with frosty ties.
In winter's dance, the spirit grows,
Among the shades of white and rose.

Windows framed in frosted art,
Nature's canvas, a stunning part.
Each delicate flake, a work of love,
The elegance from skies above.

In every shimmer, light unfolds,
A story told in hues so bold.
Together in this frozen play,
We find the art of winter's sway.

Frost-laden Whispers

Whispers of the cold wind sigh,
As snowflakes dance and softly fly.
Frosty breath hangs in the air,
A winter's tale, a heartfelt prayer.

Underneath a blanket white,
Nature's hush turns day to night.
Footsteps crunch on fields of snow,
Echoes soft, as breezes flow.

The frost weaves in a silken thread,
Across the land, a wedding spread.
Each crystal formed with gentle care,
Tells secrets that the cold winds share.

Time stands still in this wonderland,
As dreams are crafted by nature's hand.
In glimmering lights, the world takes pause,
Wrapped in enchantment, a silent cause.

Let the whispers echo deep,
In this frosty world, we leap.
Through the whispers of the night,
Frost-laden dreams take graceful flight.

Enfolded in Chill

Beneath the stars, the world is still,
Enfolded soft in winter's chill.
A blanket white, a soft caress,
In frozen silence, we confess.

The moonlight casts a silver glow,
On hills adorned with pristine snow.
Each shadow dances, softly bright,
In the embrace of velvet night.

Gentle whispers through the trees,
Nature's song, a soothing breeze.
The frosty breath of dusk arrives,
In chill wrapped dreams, the heart revives.

Stars above like scattered gems,
In this enchanted realm it seems.
We're cradled in the night so deep,
As winter holds us in its sweep.

Every flake tells tales of yore,
In each sweet moment, we explore.
The beauty found in quiet grace,
Enfolded in this chilling space.

As dawn awakens, magic fades,
Leaving traces where love cascades.
Yet in the heart, the chill remains,
A memory wrapped in winter's chains.

Milton Keynes UK
Ingram Content Group UK Ltd.
UKHW010231111224
452348UK00011B/667